Know Your Birthday Manners

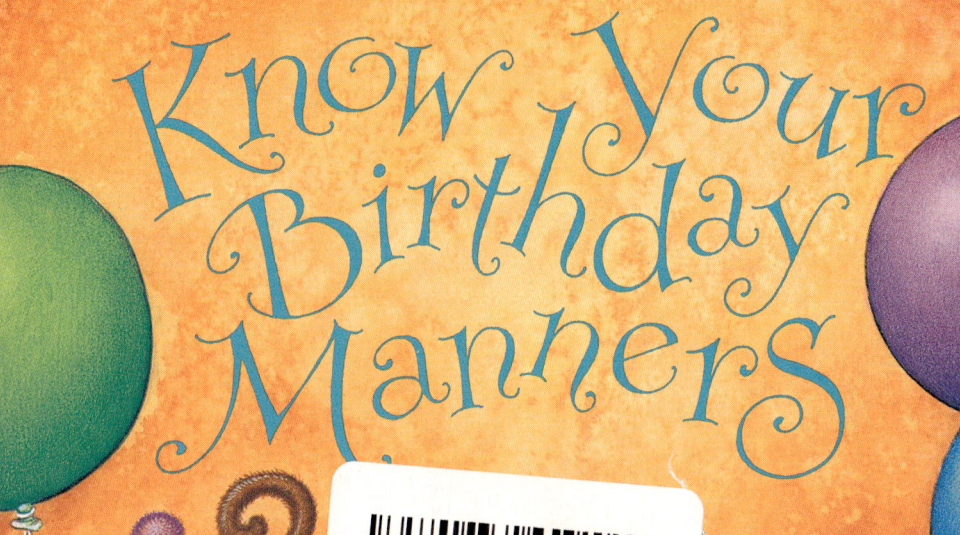

written by Clara Reiff
illustrated by Leah Palmer Preiss

HARCOURT BRACE & COMPANY

Orlando   Atlanta   Austin   Boston   San Francisco   Chicago   Dallas   New York
Toronto   London

DO NOT eat with your hands.

Please, eat with your fork.

DO NOT climb on the table.

Please, sit on the chair.

DO NOT put cake on the rug.

Please, use a plate.

DO have a happy birthday!